NEW WAYS
FOR FAMILIES®

PARENT WORKBOOK

UNHOOKED BOOKS

AN IMPRINT OF HIGH CONFLICT INSTITUTE PRESS

SCOTTSDALE ARIZONA USA

Third edition.

A Note to the Reader

This publication is designed to provide accurate and authoritative information about the subject matters covered. It is sold with the understanding that neither the author nor publisher are rendering legal, mental health, medical or other professional services, either directly or indirectly. If expert assistance, legal services or counseling is needed, the services of a competent professional should be sought. Names and identifying information of private individuals have been changed to preserve anonymity. Neither the authors nor the publisher shall be liable or responsible for any loss or damage allegedly arising as a consequence of your use or application of any information or suggestions in this book.

ISBN-13: 978-1936268054

Publisher
Unhooked Books
7701 E. Indian School Rd., Ste. F
Scottsdale, AZ 85251 USA
www.unhookedbooks.com

Ordering and Contact Information
New Ways for Families
Email: newways@highconflictinstitute.com
Website: NewWays4Families.com

Printed in the United States of America

CONTENTS

INTRODUCTION

New Ways for Families ® is a 4-Step method. The overall goal is to help both parents develop new ways of making decisions, communicating, and planning for your children in a separation or divorce. This method may be used if you voluntarily agreed or if a court ordered you to use this approach; it can also be used if you have direct contact with each other or no direct contact. You may be using this in counseling or coaching sessions with a professional, depending on your community providers.

Step 1: Getting Started includes a court order or signed agreement to use this method. You can also work on these skills with your coach/counselor voluntarily, without a court order or signed agreement.

The goals of Step 2: Individual Parent Coaching/Counseling are intended to:

1. Strengthen your skills for dealing with a potentially high-conflict other parent.

2. Strengthen skills that you will teach to your child/ren in Step 3.

3. Strengthen skills for making family decisions.

4. If you go to court, strengthen skills to avoid becoming a high-conflict parent.

Skills-Building Counseling

New Ways for Families® involves a different kind of coaching/counseling known as "skills-building." You may be familiar with counseling that focuses on the past and your feelings about the past, but this approach emphasizes the future and strengthening your skills for solving new problems when they come up. Comments about the past may be addressed briefly with your coach/counselor. The Workbook helps you and your coach/counselor look at how you can solve problems like those that may have occurred in the past by practicing the skills for avoiding or solving these problems in the future. Feel free to ask your coach/counselor about how this new approach works. Hundreds of parents have now tried this method and said that these skills were helpful for them in all aspects of their lives, not just their separation or divorce.

THIS WORKBOOK

This workbook is designed to be used during your **Step 2: Individual Parent Coaching/Counseling** sessions and **Step 3: Parent-Child Counseling** sessions. You can do some of the writing exercises between sessions; or you can do all of the writing during your sessions. Both parents are expected to work on the same skills and exercises in their own workbooks.

Step 2: Individual Coaching or Counseling

At the end of your individual coaching or counseling session, if you have attended 6 full sessions and completed all of the writing exercises, your coach/counselor will sign the verification of completion of individual parent coaching/counseling. You can provide this to the court, if requested. However, your coach/counselor is not allowed to submit a letter or declaration for the court, so that this coaching/counseling is kept confidential. (of course, there are certain standard exceptions to counselor confidentiality which still apply, such as reports of child abuse, elder abuse, etc.)

Step 3: Parent-Child Counseling

After you are finished with the individual parent coaching or counseling, you will each meet with your children three times in parent-child coaching/counseling. Preparing what to tell your children can be discussed in your individual parent coaching/counseling. The parent-child sessions are intended to give you a supportive space to teach these skills to your children and to talk about how the family will operate in the future with guidance from the professional. These sessions are not designed for discussion of the past, as the focus is on teaching and discussing skills for parents and children to be successful in the future.

Step 4: Family (or Court) Decision-Making

The last step is making family decisions for the new ways that your family is organized and how you and your co-parent can work together in the best interest of your child/ren. This includes your parenting schedule, how you will communicate, make decisions, plan activities, etc. If you and your co-parent can make these decisions on your own, then you may not need to return to court. If the two of you are unable to make these decisions, then the judge may expect you to explain what you have learned from your individual counseling and parent-child counseling sessions before he or she makes these important decisions for you and your family.

INDIVIDUAL PARENT COACHING/ COUNSELING

SESSION 1: Setting your goals

High-conflict separations and divorces are getting a lot of attention these days, because they can cost parents a lot of money, cost courts a lot of time, and cost children a lot of harm to their long-term mental health. Reducing the conflict has become a goal of many government legislatures and the courts.

Families in high-conflict often have some or all of the following four characteristics:

All-or-nothing thinking
Unmanaged emotions
Extreme behaviors
Preoccupation with blaming others

In many families, only one parent has these high-conflict characteristics and the other parent is trying hard to be reasonable and protect the child/ren. In other families, both parents have some of these characteristics, although one may be more extreme than the other. To avoid these four characteristics, this Individual Parent Coaching/Counseling is designed to strengthen your skills in four main areas:

Flexible Thinking
Managed Emotions
Moderate Behaviors
Checking Yourself

By practicing these skills, you may be able to influence the other parent to use them as well, or you will at least be able to show the court that you are not acting in a high-conflict manner.

The first session is focused on setting goals to help you apply these skills to your own situation. The following are the four General Goals and you can think up the Specific Goals to go under each one:

1. To use flexible thinking in dealing with the other parent.
2. To manage upset emotions during the separation or divorce.
3. To use moderate behaviors with the other parent and children.
4. To validate my own strengths and personal qualities.
5. To "check myself" during times of stress, before reacting to a situation or to the behaviors of the other parent

Here's a list of possible Specific Goals:

"To practice flexible thinking when my partner/spouse is blaming me."

"To manage my emotions when the children criticize my actions."

"To respond with moderate behaviors when my partner/spouse sends angry emails."

"To get my partner/spouse to listen to me when I make parenting suggestions."

"To protect my children from the other parent's comments and behavior.

If the court has ordered you to address specific behaviors, see where they fit into these goals and show your coach/counselor a copy of the court order. If the other parent has requested that you address specific issues, and you agree, see if they might fit in as goals as well.

After discussing these ideas with your coach/counselor, write a Specific Goal under each General Goal:

1. **To use flexible thinking in dealing with the other parent.**

    My specific goal:

    _____

2. **To manage upset emotions during the separation or divorce.**

    My specific goal:

    _____

3. **To use moderate behaviors with the other parent and children.**

    My specific goals:

    _____

4. **To "check myself" during times of stress before reacting to the situation or behavior of the other parent.**

    My specific goal:

    _____

5. **To validate my own strengths and personal qualities.**

    My specific goal:

    _____

Throughout *New Ways for Families*®, you and your coach/counselor can look back on your goals to see if you are learning what you want to learn. You can change or add to these goals if something more meaningful comes up in the coaching/counseling sessions. The goals are meant to guide you, not rule your life. But remember, these are your goals, so make sure to bring them up in your discussions of the skills described in this manual each week.

Also, throughout *New Ways for Families*®, hurdles will come up that get in the way of meeting your Specific Goals. This is natural when we practice skills or change how we do things.

Write two or three hurdles that might get in the way of meeting your goals. **After discussing these hurdles with your coach/counselor**, write down how you might deal with these hurdles.

HURDLES TO NEW WAYS FOR FAMILIES	WAYS OF DEALING WITH THEM
_____	_____
_____	_____
_____	_____
_____	_____

Examples:

I don't have time to do the written homework. I can do the homework in the waiting room, or with my coach/counselor during our session.

My mind goes blank on things like this.	I can discuss this with my coach/counselor. I can ask other people for suggestions.
I don't want to do this coaching/counseling.	I don't have to like it. I can just do it. I might learn something anyway.
My dog will eat my homework.	I can keep my Workbook at my coach/counselor's office and work on it before the sessions.
I'm a perfectionist and I'm afraid I won't do it right.	There's no "right way" in New Ways for Families.

All you have to do is talk and write about flexible thinking, managing emotions, behaving in close relationships, recognizing your own strengths and practicing moderate behaviors in response to difficult situations. Remember, being flexible and doing things differently can be one of your Specific Goals.

Discuss your strengths and positive qualities with your coach/counselor. After discussing these, write down some specific strengths and positive qualities that you have. Let your coach/counselor help you write these in purely positive terms:

_____

_____

_____

_____

Give your coach/counselor some background history on your family situation and answer any questions your coach/counselor might ask. Also, when describing your family situation, describe examples of when you or someone else used all-or-nothing thinking, unmanaged emotions, and/or extreme behaviors. Write one or more examples here:

_____

_____

Discuss homework with your coach/counselor that you could do before your next coaching/counseling session to strengthen your awareness of all-or-nothing thinking, unmanaged emotions, and extreme behaviors by yourself or others. (Be careful not to point these out to other people or they may become very defensive, whether you are accurate or not.)

And that's it. You're done with Session #1. Congratulations!

Session 2: Calming upset emotions

As we face new situations in this rapidly changing world, there are many times that we will feel upset. If you are going through a divorce, a job change, a move or any other change, you know what we are talking about. You might feel confused. Or worried. Or angry. Or sad. Yet upset feelings are just feelings and can be managed. Emotions are normal and we all have lots of them.

The goal isn't to eliminate feelings. The goal is to understand what we are feeling and to make decisions about which feelings to act on and which feelings to set aside; which feelings to show and which feelings to hide. Feelings are information which may help us, if we *think* before we act. But what do we do with the feelings that are *so* upsetting?

Before your meet with your coach/counselor, if possible, or with your coach/counselor:

Think of a time when your upset feelings helped you solve a problem and write it down:

_____

_____

Think of when your upset feelings got in the way of solving a problem, or created a problem:

_____

_____

Discuss both of the above situations with your coach/counselor.

There are many methods of calming upset emotions.

1. **Take a Break**

    One of the most successful ways of calming down is to take a break. This can mean excusing yourself from an angry conversation for a few minutes. "Let me just stop and think for a few minutes." "Let's discuss this later." "I just need some time to think."

Before you meet with your coach/counselor, if possible, or with your coach/counselor:

Write down a situation when you took a break and it helped you calm down:

_____

_____

_____

Write down a situation that might occur in the future, when you might need to take a break:

_____

_____

_____

Write down what you could say in the situation above, so that you could take a break:

_____

_____

Discuss the above situations with your coach/counselor. After discussing these situations, write down another situation where you might need to take a break, and what you could say or do.

_____

_____

_____

Practice saying you need a break with your coach/counselor playing someone in your life. Discuss how it felt to say that.

2. **Talk to someone neutral.**

Separation or divorce is often very upsetting times. When we get upset, it often helps to talk to someone else about it. If possible, it is best to talk to someone who will stay out of the conflict and just lend an ear, so that they don't make things worse for you. Pick someone and call them or visit them and say: "I just need someone to listen for a few minutes. Are you available?"

Think of three people you could call when you are upset:

1. _____

2. _____

3. _____

3. Tell yourself encouraging statements

In the Olympics, most of the athletes learn to tell themselves encouraging statements while they are in the middle of extremely difficult challenges—especially when things are going badly and they are feeling very stressed or upset. These statements help them keep their cool.

Before meeting with your coach/counselor, if possible, or with your coach/counselor:

Think of three encouraging statements anyone can tell themselves to get through a hard time:

For example: "You can do it!"

1. _____

2. _____

3. _____

Think of three encouraging statements specific to you, that you can tell yourself in an upset time:

For example: "Remember, I got through a worse situation last year! I'll get through this too!"

1. _____

2. _____

3. _____

Discuss the above statements with your coach/counselor. See if you can come up with two more, after discussing the above.

4. _____

5. _____

Use flexible thinking

Flexible thinking can also help you calm your upset feelings. For example, if you are upset that your child "never listens" to you, think of a time that your child has listened to you. It's not "all or never," although it may feel that way sometimes. Think of a statement that has flexible thinking in it, that could help you calm your upset emotions in a future situation:

_____

_____

When things go badly, focus on the future and what you can do. Put your energy into flexible thinking to find a good solution if it happens again. For example, if the other parent comes late to pick up the children, think of two or three ways you could deal with that in the future, such as: agreeing that you can leave with the children and arrange a later exchange time; have a financial penalty for late pickups (like $5 for 15 or more minutes); or changing the next pickup to a later time. Just thinking that you have options can calm you down.

Practice a situation with your coach/counselor in which you might get upset this coming week. First, practice with you being the upsetting person saying the upsetting things, and let your coach/counselor be you, saying what you could say in response. Then, practice with your coach/counselor being the upsetting person saying the upsetting things, and you practice responding.

Write down what you want to remember from this practice exercise, so you can remember to use it this week if the situation comes up.

_____

_____

Calming Yourself While Writing Emails

BIFF Responses

Read the article "Responding to Hostile Mail (B.I.F.F.)" in <u>Appendix A</u> on page 50. Discuss the way that Jane calmed down and responded to Joe.

Then, do the following writing exercise.

Email Exercise #1

Eric and Connie

Write a B.I.F.F. response for Eric to Connie based on the email exchange below:

Eric: "I'd like to have Wally on Tuesday evening, June 14th, to attend a father-son baseball game that our group has organized. I know it's usually your night, but I'd like to have this night. I'm willing to switch with another night, in order to be flexible."

Connie: "Eric, you have not been helping Wally enough with his homework on his school nights! I will end your weekday overnights if you don't spend at least two hours helping him study on both of your weekday parenting nights. I want you to keep a record of the exact hours that he spends studying while he is at your house. You know I thought this parenting arrangement wouldn't work out, and it hasn't!!! And you know it!!!"

Eric: "_____

_____

_____

_____

_____

_____ "

Discuss your response with your coach /counselor.

If you have time, do the Optional Email Exercise following the BIFF article on page 50.

Discuss your response with your coach /counselor.

If you have time, discuss the following examples with your coach/counselor:

A.   Mary just found out that Jim is going to be an hour late to pick up the children. She was going to leave to see a movie with a friend after they were picked up, so now she'll miss it. She is very upset. What could she do to calm her upset emotions?

B.   Jim feels very controlled by Mary. Now she is on the phone telling him she wants to cancel his parenting time because the children have extra homework tonight that is due tomorrow. He is very upset. How could he tell her he needs to take a break to calm down and think? What could he say to himself before he responds to her?

C.   Frank has just threatened over the phone to take Susan back to court to fight for a change of custody, because their daughter is resisting spending time with him this weekend. Susan is very upset to hear this. How could she tell him she needs to take a break to calm down and think? What could she say to herself before she responds to him?

D.   Sarah has enrolled their son in soccer in her neighborhood without discussing it with Fred. She just told him as she was dropping off the children. He is furious. What can he do to calm his emotions? What could he say to himself before he responds to her?

E.   **Read the article** "Positive and Negative Advocates" in <u>Appendix B</u> on page 53. Discuss this article with your coach/counselor.

Circle the word that best describes today's counseling session.

Perfect   Good   Okay   So-So   Not good   Terrible

Explain your choice to your coach/counselor, and one idea to make the next session better.

End of Session #2

SESSION 3: Flexible thinking

We are constantly facing new situations that may never have occurred in our lives before, or even in the world before. One of the biggest barriers to success in a changing world is all-or-nothing thinking. What we need is flexible thinking for new ways of solving problems in new situations. All-or-nothing thinking keeps us stuck in old ways, while flexible thinking helps us keep thinking of new ideas and trying them out until something works. Here are some common examples of all-or-nothing thinking:

"My life isn't working. I have to change everything that I do."

"The divorce is all his/her fault. There is nothing I need to do differently."

"The divorce is all my fault. I might as well give up trying."

"Everyone is against me. The judge, the attorneys, the mediator. There's nothing I can do."

"Everyone will see things my way: the judge, attorneys, mediator. I can't wait to tell them."

"I'm perfect as I am. There is nothing I can learn from this coach/counselor."

"Everything I do is wrong. This coach/counselor will save me."

Write two *realistic* statements that are not "all-or-nothing thinking" that relate to your life:

For example: "I can learn new ways of doing things, regardless of how I did things in the past."

Or: "My partner/spouse may be able to change some of his/her parenting behavior. Let's see."

1. _____

_____

2. _____

_____

Someone You Know

Think of someone in your life who often uses all-or-nothing thinking. Write two examples of what he/she would say or think:

1. _____

_____

2. _____

_____

Write two new flexible ways that he/she could speak or think in the future on these subjects:

1. _____

_____

_____

2. _____

_____

_____

Remember, this is just a practice exercise to help you learn new ways of flexible thinking. So don't really tell the other person to think differently. That's their job. Focus on yourself now.

Yourself

Think of two examples of all-or-nothing thinking that you have sometimes. Write them here:

1. _____

_____

2. _____

_____

Write flexible ways that you could speak or think differently from what you wrote above:

1. _____

_____

2. _____

_____

Discuss with your coach/counselor why you think that flexible thinking is helpful or unhelpful, or in what types of situations it could be helpful or unhelpful. Write an example of when flexible thinking could be helpful in your family situation now:

_____

_____

_____

Discuss with your coach/counselor two statements you can practice to remind yourself to use flexible thinking in the future, and situations where you plan to practice them this week. Write them here. Keep them short and easy to remember.

1. _____

_____

2. _____

_____

Making Proposals

Read the article "Making Proposals" in <u>Appendix C</u> to this Workbook (it explains a moderate approach to making proposals to your former partner/spouse). Discuss with your coach/counselor. Then, together practice reading the script in the Proposal Exercise that follows the article, with your coach/counselor playing the part of Natasha and yourself playing the part of William. Then have a similar practice dialog with your coach/counselor using a decision you are facing in your case. Making proposals is a very helpful skill to develop for use in your case and anywhere.

If you have time, discuss the following examples with your coach/counselor.

A. Joe was 5 minutes late picking up the children for his weekend, so Mary decided that she would leave and take them shopping with her for the next few hours. Was that all-or-nothing thinking? If so, what could Mary have done that shows flexible thinking? What could Joe do that shows flexible thinking?

B. Alicia is not good at math. In discussing their parenting schedule, Robert proposes that she only have parenting time on Saturdays, so that he can help their son with math on weekdays and Sundays. Does his proposal show all-or-nothing thinking? If so, what could Robert do to show flexible thinking? How could Alicia respond with flexible thinking?

C. Ellen thinks that the children do not need their father in their life now that they are separated. She and her mother can raise their children just fine without him, she thinks. Is this all-or-nothing thinking? If so, what would be flexible thinking for Ellen?

D. Jack thinks that the children should have no contact with their mother, since she is depressed sometimes and cut her wrists once in a suicide attempt two years ago. Is this all-or-nothing thinking? If so, what would be flexible thinking for Jack?

Circle the word that best describes today's coaching/counseling session.

Perfect   Good   Okay   So-So   Not good   Terrible

Explain your choice to your coach/counselor, and one idea to make the next session better.

End of Session #3

Session 4: Feelings are contagious

Feelings are contagious. Recent brain research has shown this. If someone is feeling happy, others around him or her will start to feel happier too. If someone is feeling sad, those nearby may also feel sad feelings. Sometimes people pressure us to have the same feeling they are having, especially when they are angry.

Before you meet with your coach/counselor, if possible, or with your coach/counselor:

Write two situations in which someone wanted you to feel the same way they felt:

1. _____

_____

2. _____

_____

Describe to your coach/counselor how it felt to have someone pressure you to have the same feeling that they were having. Explain how you handled the situation. (Did you have the same feeling?)

Write down how you would have preferred that the other person handled the situation.

1. _____

_____

2. _____

_____

Write two situations in which you pressured someone to feel the same as you felt (we all have):

1. _____

_____

2. _____

_____

Discuss with your coach/counselor why you wanted them to feel the same way as you did. Discuss whether they agreed with you or whether they just said what you wanted to hear because of your pressure. Discuss another way you could have dealt with the situation.

Describe to your coach/counselor a situation when you picked up the same feelings another person had, without either of you realizing it until afterwards. (For example, yawning soon after a baby yawned.)

Write down two examples of when you picked up the feeling another person was having, and when you realized it.

1. _____

_____

2. _____

_____

Discuss with your coach/counselor how you can become aware sooner of picking up someone else's feelings, moods, or behaviors.

Think of 3 things you can tell yourself to help you avoid picking up other people's feelings without realizing it:

1. _____

_____

2. _____

_____

3. _____

_____

Your children may pick up your upset feelings during a separation or divorce. This is very common. It is the same effect when we are at the movies and feel angry or sad along with the main characters. The more attached we are to the character, the more we feel what the character feels. For children, parents are like a movie – as they observe you, they will feel some of what you are feeling.

For example, if you are angry at your partner/spouse in front of your children, they are more likely to become angry at your partner/spouse as well. Or if you are sad as they leave to spend time with the other parent, they will feel sad as well. Recent brain research on mirror neurons is starting to explain how this happens. It is usually unconscious and may be unavoidable if children are within sight or hearing of their parents when they are intensely upset.

How can you protect your children from your upset emotions during the separation or divorce process? There are several ways, which especially include keeping your intensely upset emotions about the other parent out of sight and hearing of the children.

A. Out of sight and hearing:

List three ways you can keep your intense emotions out of sight and hearing of your child/ren:

1. _____

2. _____

3. _____

B. Regularly make positive comments:

Regular positive comments about the other parent build resilience against any negative statements and emotions that the children see and hear. List three positive qualities of the other parent that you can say regularly to your child/ren:

1. _____

2. _____

3. _____

C. Make "repairing" comments:

Repairing comments are made in any relationship when people say negative things and then say they are sorry and didn't mean to be so negative. For example, you could say: "I just said something very negative about your other parent and I didn't mean to be so negative. He/she has many positive qualities and my feelings are my responsibility, not his/hers and not yours. Sorry about that."

List three negative statements you have made about the other parent with emotional intensity in front of your child/ren (everyone does this sometimes, even when couples live together). Then write a repairing comment for each that you could make if it happens again in the future.

1. Negative Statement: _____

_____

Repairing Comment: _____

_____

2. Negative Statement: _____

_____

Repairing Comment: _____

_____

3. Negative Statement: _____

_____

Repairing Comment: _____

_____

Discuss with your coach/counselor a situation that could come up this week in which you could protect your child/ren from your negative emotions about the other parent. Practice what you could say or do with your coach/counselor.

Read the article "Is Your Child Alienated?" in Appendix D on page 59 after this session (it explains more about repairing comments).

Circle the word that best describes today's coaching/counseling session.

Perfect   Good   Okay   So-So   Not good   Terrible

Explain your choice to your coach/counselor, and one idea to make the next session better.

End of Session #4

Session 5: Feelings aren't decisions

We are always having feelings. Sometimes they are positive and sometimes they are negative. As was said in the last two sessions, the goal isn't to eliminate feelings. The goal is to understand what we are feeling and to make decisions about which feelings to act on and which feelings to set aside; which feelings to show and which feelings to hide. Feelings are information which may help us, if we *think* before we act.

Where do feelings come from? They come from many sources, including (but not limited to):

Our biological needs (hunger, fear of danger, natural drive to be close to people, natural drive to be independent, etc.)

Our life experiences (that certain people are appealing, certain people are dangerous, etc.)

Our self-esteem (how we feel about our appearance, our feelings about money, styles, etc.)

Our moods of the day (hard day at work, child threw up, good friend cheered us up, etc.)

Before you meet with your coach/counselor, if possible, or when you meet with your coach/counselor:

Write down three situations in which you often feel sad; often feel angry; and often feel happy:

1.   Sad: _____

            _____

2.   Angry: _____

            _____

3.   Happy: _____

            _____

Discuss each situation briefly with your coach/counselor. Discuss whether or not you know what you are feeling while you are *in* each situation above. Discuss whether you ever changed how you felt in one of these situations (like you felt sad, then cheered yourself up a little; or felt angry and calmed yourself down).

Should you just do it?

Our feelings are significantly influenced by our culture. For example:

> In the 1960's, Janis Joplin said "If it feels good, do it!"

> In the 1970's, Luke Skywalker of Star Wars was told "Go with your feelings!"

> In the 1990's, an advertisement said "Just do it!"

> In the 2000's, an advertisement says "Obey your thirst!"

All of these sayings teach people to act on their feelings without thinking – to act impulsively.

Discuss with your coach/counselor whether you think the above sayings are always a good idea, always a bad idea, or sometimes a good idea. Remember flexible thinking. Describe one situation when they might apply and one situation where they would not apply:

1. _____

_____

2. _____

_____

Think of two situations when you have done what you felt like doing and regretted it afterwards:

1. _____

_____

2. _____

_____

Discuss with your coach/counselor what you learned from those experiences:

1. _____

_____

2. _____

_____

Extreme Behaviors

Extreme behaviors are most often driven by extreme feelings. Extreme behaviors include hitting people, hitting children, hiding money, lying, etc. Often people regret using extreme behaviors after their extreme feelings have calmed down. Think of two extreme behaviors that you regretted after you calmed down your upset emotions:

1. _____

_____

2. _____

_____

Now, think of two situations where you felt like doing an extreme behavior, but did a moderate behavior instead. Write the behavior you *felt* like doing, then write what you actually did. Then write how you felt about it afterwards: if you were glad or not that you used moderate behavior.

1.   What I felt like doing: _____

        What I did: _____

        How I felt about it afterwards: _____

2.   What I felt like doing: _____

        What I did: _____

        How I felt about it afterwards: _____

Think of a situation in the coming week when you might feel like doing an extreme behavior. Write the situation and a moderate behavior you could use instead:

Situation: _____

_____

Moderate behavior: _____

_____

Should children just do what they feel?

Discuss with your coach/counselor what types of decisions children should make and what types of decisions they shouldn't make. Make a list of each:

DECISIONS CHILDREN SHOULD MAKE	DECISIONS THEY SHOULD NOT MAKE
1. _____	1. _____
_____	_____
2. _____	2. _____
_____	_____
3. _____	3. _____
_____	_____

For the decisions that children should make on the left above, describe the role that feelings should play in making each of those types of decisions. For example, if a child wanted to play on the soccer team, but felt that he or she would be embarrassed, would that be a good reason to decide not to play? For another example, if a teenager felt like kissing a boy or girl, would that be a good reason to just do it?

ROLE OF FEELINGS IN MAKING THE DECISIONS ABOVE ON THE LEFT:

_____

_____

_____

_____

For the decisions that children should not make on the right above, describe the age at which they should be able to decide these things:

_____

_____

_____

_____

Checking Yourself

Having all of these skills won't do you any good, unless you regularly check yourself to see if you're using them. In a stressful situation, we often forget to use the skills that will help us the most. So whenever a new decision-making situation with your co-parent pops up, ask yourself these questions:

1. How can I use my **_flexible thinking_** to deal with this situation? Should I make a proposal?

2. How can I **_manage my emotions_** in this situation? Can I give myself encouraging statements? Or remove myself briefly from the situation?

3. How can I use **_moderate behaviors_** right now? Should I communicate using a BIFF Response?

It's also helpful to ask yourself these questions when you are thinking too much about the other person's behavior. It's easy for us to decide that someone else needs to manage themselves better, because it's harder for us to manage ourselves. Yet managing yourself may actually have a positive influence on the other person. For example, if you send enough BIFF Responses, some people may start responding to you with BIFF Responses – because they learned it from you! You can't control other people, but sometimes you can influence them.

Write three types of situations where it might help you to Check Yourself and use these skills in the next few weeks:

1. _____

2. _____

3. _____

New Ways of Making Decisions

Now that you and your partner/spouse are separated or divorced, it will be very important for your children that the two of you make good decisions for them. The next session is the last meeting of these 6 sessions of Individual Parent Coaching or Counseling. You and your partner/spouse can decide whether or not you want to make this last session a joint session with both of you and both of your coaches/counselors. If you do not want this last session to be a joint session with you and your co-parent, then you will each complete this final session with your own coach/counselor. It's only a joint session if both parents agree, without any pressure to meet jointly. The session (joint or separate) will focus on what your children can learn from each of you and the new ways you want to make decisions in the future for your children's benefit.

Write the reasons it would be a good idea for you and your partner/spouse to meet together at the next meeting:

_____

_____

_____

Write the reasons it would not be a good idea for the two of you to meet together at this session:

_____

_____

_____

Discuss with our coach/counselor whether you and your partner/spouse should meet together or not. Avoid basing your decision on extreme feelings. There is no right or wrong answer.

Make arrangements for the last session. Whether or not it is going to be a joint session, think about and write your proposed decisions about the following before the last session:

1. How you propose communicating with each other (such as by email, phone, etc.):

_____

_____

2. The types of decisions that you should make jointly for your child/ren's best interests:

_____

_____

3. The types of decisions that you should make separately for your child/ren:

_____

_____

4. The types of decisions that your child/ren can make:

_____

_____

Read the article "Don't Use Force" in Appendix E on page 61 after this session (it explains more about how parents' emotions can influence their children's behavior).

Circle the word that best describes today's coaching/counseling session.

Perfect   Good   Okay   So-So   Not good   Terrible

Explain your choice to your coach/counselor, and one idea to make the next session better.

End of Session #5

Session 6: Learning from both parents

(If this is a session with both parents and both coaches/counselors, jointly proceed with the discussions and exercises in this Workbook and schedule a second joint session if needed.)

To be resilient in today's world, your children need to learn many points of view and many ways of doing things. They need to be able to learn that people are different, and to learn different ways of coping with different people, including total jerks. The first and most important people to learn these lessons from are their parents, even during adolescence. They are learning all the time from both of you, even when you don't realize it. They learn good things that help and bad things that don't help, or even hurt them. Nobody's perfect, so we need to keep learning.

Before you meet with your coach(es)/counselor(s):

Think of three good things that your child/ren have learned from you:

_____

_____

_____

Think of three good things that you hope to teach your child/ren in the future:

_____

_____

_____

Think of three good things that your child/ren have learned from the other parent:

_____

_____

_____

Think of three good things that you hope the other parent will teach your child/ren in the future:

_____

_____

_____

When you meet with your coach(es)/counselor(s):

Think of two good things that you learned from your parent(s) that you still do:

What I learned from Parent 1:

_____

_____

What I learned from Parent 2:

_____

_____

Think of two things your parent(s) taught you that were not helpful and that you don't do or try not to do:

From Parent 1:

_____

_____

From Parent 2:

_____

_____

Discuss all of the above with your coach(es)/counselor(s).

Write something you learned from discussing the above with your coach(es)counselor(s):

_____

_____

_____

_____

Discuss with your coach(es)/counselor(s), then write down:

Two ways that the other parent could support you in teaching your child good skills:

_____

_____

Two ways that you could support the other parent in teaching your child good skills:

_____

_____

If your child is resisting contact with one of you, discuss with your coach(es)/counselor(s):

Two things you could say to help strengthen your child's relationship with the other parent:

1. _____

2. _____

Two things you could *do* to help strengthen your child's relationship with the other parent:

1. _____

2. _____

Write two problems that will arise if there are changes in your child's schedule between your two homes:

1. _____

2. _____

Write how you can help your child overcome these hurdles:

1. _____

2. _____

Preparing for the Parent-Child Counseling

(If this is a joint session, jointly make plans for Step 3: Parent-Child Counseling. If you both agree, the last session of the Parent-Child Counseling can be a joint session with both of you and your child/ren. The first two sessions each should be with you alone with the child/ren.)

To assist the children and yourself in beginning the Parent-Child Counseling, you may wish to prepare an initial statement to your children at the first Parent-Child session that includes the following issues. An example is in "The New Ways Parent-Child Talk" in Appendix F (**p.   **). Many parents find that it helps to write this out in your own words before the first Parent-Child session.

1. New ways in different houses

2. Positive ways with each other

3. Avoiding extreme behaviors

4. Managing our emotions

5. Emotions can be contagious

6. Flexible thinking

7. Rules in both houses

Conclusion (With your individual coach/counselor)

This is the last part of Step 2, the first 6 sessions of *New Ways for Families*®. Discuss with your coach/counselor what you have learned regarding each of your four specific goals that you set in Session #1..

1. **To use flexible thinking in dealing with the other parent.**

My specific goal: _____

What I learned: _____

2. **To manage upset emotions during the separation or divorce.**

My specific goal: _____

What I learned: _____

3.   **To use moderate behaviors with the other parent and children.**

My specific goal: _____

What I learned: _____

4.   **To check myself on a regular basis.**

My specific goal: _____

What I learned: _____

5.   **To validate my own strengths and personal qualities.**

My specific goal: _____

What I learned: _____

Write one thing you would like to learn in the future, and how you could learn it:

_____

_____

_____

CONGRATULATIONS!

You have completed Step 2 of *New Ways for Families*.

INTRODUCTION

Parent-Child Counseling

New Ways for Families® is a 4-step program. The Parent-Child Counseling occurs after you have completed Step 2: Individual Parent Counseling. After <u>both</u> parents have completed Individual Parent Counseling, you are ready to begin Step 3: Parent-Child Counseling.

Step 3: Parent-Child Counseling

You and the other parent will each meet three times with your child/ren and the Parent-Child Counselor. You should alternate sessions (ideally, alternating weeks with the other parent), so that the children hear the same basic messages from each of you, and so each of you hears similar concerns from your children. With three meetings each, this whole Step should be completed in approximately 6 -8 weeks.

Who Meets First?

Which parent meets first with your child/ren can be based on schedules and preferences of the parents. If the child currently prefers one parent and resists contact with the other parent, or the child has had no contact with one parent for a while, the first parent to meet with the child should be the "preferred" parent. This parent can discuss support for the child meeting with the other parent. Then you should still alternate sessions. Neither parent should have their second session until both parents have had their first session, and the third session should not occur until both have had their second session.

Optional Joint Session

If both parents agree that it would be beneficial to meet jointly with the child/ren for the third session of Parent-Child Counseling, then discuss the details of arranging this session with your Parent-Child Counselor. But there should be no pressure, so if one parent prefers not to meet jointly then it should be done separately by each parent with the child/ren.

Goals of Step 3

1. Assist you in teaching your children skills for resilience in the separation or divorce.
2. Assist you in hearing your children's concerns about the separation or divorce.
3. Assist you in discussing new activities and new decision-making for your children.
4. Assist you and the other parent in discussing new ways for your family with the children, *if you meet jointly with the other parent and the children.*
5. Observe your interactions and answer the judge's questions about your parenting skills, *if you go to court.*

Non-Confidential Counseling

The Parent-Child Counseling is designed to be non-confidential, so that the Counselor may talk with other professionals involved in the case, if you, as the parents, agree it would be beneficial. This usually means that the parents should sign consents at the beginning of the Parent-Child Counseling allowing the Parent-Child Counselor to speak to a mediator or other professionals involved in the case. The Parent-Child Counselor should not make recommendations to the court nor write a report. The ideal goal is to assist you, as the parents, in developing and practicing skills that will help you resolve any case decisions out of court by agreement, such as with the assistance of a mediator or lawyers. The purpose of the Parent-Child Counseling is solely to assist the parents and children in learning and practicing the skills, not evaluating the parents. Ideally the Parent-Child Counselor will be available to answer questions from other professionals about the Counselor's observations of the counseling, without asking for or giving recommendations or expert opinions.

This Workbook Section

Each parent will complete the Parent-Child Counseling section of this Parent Workbook. You will use this during the sessions with your child. You will write what your child says in response to certain questions. There is nothing that your child will be expected to write. You can keep your Parent Workbook, but your Parent-Child Counselor will need to see that you have completed the Parent-Child Counseling section in order to sign the verification at the end of the Workbook. As the Parent-Child Counseling is not confidential, the Parent-Child Counseling section of this Workbook *may not* be confidential if you go to court.

Step 4: Family (or Court) Decision-Making

After you complete Parent-Child Counseling, the last step is making family decisions for the new ways that your family is organized. This includes:

        Your parenting schedule

        How to change the parenting schedule

        Taking a parenting class separately or together

        How you will communicate

        How you will jointly make decisions

        How you will separately make decisions

        How you will plan child activities

        How other people (relatives, new partners) are included in your child's lives

If you and the other parent can make these decisions on your own, then you may not need to return to court. You can use mediation, collaborative divorce, negotiating attorneys, or others to assist you in making these decisions.

If You Go to Court

If the court has ordered you to complete this program and the two of you are unable to make these decisions, then the judge may expect you to explain what you have learned from your Individual Coaching/Counseling and Parent-Child Counseling before he or she makes these important decisions for you

Decisions the judge makes could include: Your parenting schedule; who can change your parenting schedule and how; what parenting classes you will take separately; how or whether you will communicate directly; who will make medical, educational, extracurricular, and other decisions; whether there will be a custody evaluation or psychological evaluation; whether there will be restraining orders; whether a parent will attend a batterers treatment program; whether a parent will attend an alcohol or drug treatment program or meetings; etc.

Of course, you can jointly make these same decisions and submit them to court in a signed stipulation. The Parent-Child Counseling may help you plan how to handle these issues.

PARENT-CHILD COUNSELING

Session 1: Teaching Your Child Skills for Resiliency

Purpose of Parent-Child Counseling

The purpose of the Parent-Child Counseling is to teach your child the four big skills for life: *flexible thinking, managed emotions, moderate behaviors* and *checking yourself*; to hear your child's concerns about the separation or divorce in an open and caring manner; and to discuss new ways of doing things in your family. You will not be asked to – nor allowed to – discuss your legal case with the Parent-Child Counselor. *Mentioning criticisms of the other parent or asking the Parent-Child Counselor to act on your behalf or the child's behalf is not appropriate.*

This is not the time for decisions, but rather the time for skills – for you and your children. The goal is for you and your co-parent to be able to use your children's input and your skills *after the counseling* to reach your own decisions for the unique circumstances of your family, with the assistance of out-of-court professionals.

Before the First Parent-Child Session

Your Parent-Child Counselor should speak to you over the phone to schedule your first session and briefly explain how the Parent-Child Counseling should go. The Counselor will also explain that you should prepare the New Ways Parent-Child Talk to have at the start of the first session with your child/ren. A sample of this Talk is in your Workbook as Appendix D. It's recommended that you write down the key points you want to make in this statement in advance, or even writing out everything you want to say.

Introducing Your Child to Parent-Child Counseling

In the first session of New Ways Parent-Child Counseling, you are the teacher. The Parent-Child Counselor is there to help you and your child understand each other, and to assist you as needed in explaining these skills to your child. If you have more than one child, you and the counselor can decide whether to have shorter separate meetings with each child during this session or to meet with them together.

Explain to your child/ren that the Parent-Child Counselor is here to help you and your child/ren in discussing difficult issues and learning new skills. Tell your child/ren that you will be meeting with the child/ren and the counselor three times together. This is the same counselor who will be meeting with your child/ren and the other parent three times. These skills are so important that they need to learn them from both parents.

Explain to your child/ren that this meeting is about teaching new lessons about life which will help them throughout their lives. These are lessons about dealing with change and about handling close relationships. Tell them that you are going to teach them about *flexible thinking*, *managing emotions*, *trying new behaviors* and *checking yourself for using these skills when you're upset*, so that they can be resilient during your separation or divorce.

Explain that no one is perfect at these things, and that you are going to help them learn these things in the months and years to come. This is just a start. Tell them that you are also learning these new ways and how to use them in your own life, at work, with neighbors, and in your family and friendships.

The New Ways Parent-Child Talk

At this point, give your child a reassuring statement about your positive intentions as you and the other parent organize your family in new ways given the separation or divorce. You can use the statement in <u>Appendix F</u> on page 63 or the one you have written down for yourself.

_____

_____

_____

Flexible Thinking

Start teaching these skills by explaining flexible thinking to your child. Explain how it is different from all-or-nothing thinking. Explain that when there's a lot of changes people often have all-or-nothing thinking about what will happen, and worry about whether things will be all-good or all-bad. In reality, change is mostly what you make of it.

With flexible thinking, you can both make it better and better as you go along. If one idea doesn't work, you can try another. And if you talk about it together, you can come up with new ideas. Change can bring new opportunities you never had before, and you can learn new things you never knew before.

Tell your child two examples of times when you used flexible thinking in your life and how it was helpful to you.

Write them down here:

1. _____

_____

2. _____

_____

Then, ask your child to give you two examples of how flexible thinking helped somebody they know. If your child can't think of anything, help out by suggesting two shared memories that you and your child both know about. Write them here:

1. _____

_____

2. _____

_____

If flexible thinking triggers an important good discussion with your children, stay with your discussion. The other two basic skills below can be saved for the beginning of the next session. Otherwise, explain Managing Emotions next.

Managing Emotions

Explain new ways for your children to manage upset emotions. Explain how upset emotions are normal in new situations no matter where you are, who you are, or who you are with. Tell your child how they can *take a break* when they have upset emotions to calm themselves down. Explain how giving themselves *encouraging words* can help them calm down and manage their emotions.

Give an example of a situation in which you had upset emotions and how you were able to calm yourself down. Write the example here:

_____

_____

Ask your child to describe a situation in which they had upset emotions and how they calmed down their own emotions. Write it down here:

_____

_____

Practice what you would say to your child when you need to take a break. Practice having your child tell you that they need to take a break to calm down. If there is an important issue to discuss, tell your child it's okay to take a break for a while, as long as you get back together to discuss the important issue. Have each of you practice saying: "I need to take a break for an hour (or a day), then let's talk about this again."

Give your child an example of how you reduced the intensity of your upset emotions so that others were protected from these intense emotions. Write the example here:

_____

_____

Ask your child for an example of how they you managed their upset emotions so that someone else was protected from the intensity of these emotions. Write the example here:

_____

_____

If your child can't think of an example, try to help them remember a time when you remember that he or she reduced the intensity of their emotions to protect others. Or think of a future situation where it might be a good idea for your child to do this.

[If you are teaching Managing Emotions at the beginning of your second session, skip Moderate Behaviors for now and go to Session 2: Hearing Your Child's Concerns. If necessary, save Moderate Behaviors for your third session with your child.]

Moderate Behaviors

Explain to your child why it is helpful to use moderate behaviors, especially in new situations. Explain how extreme behaviors can make things worse, then you have to spend a lot of time trying to fix the damage of extreme behaviors. Explain how extreme behavior *in response to someone else's extreme behavior* just makes things worse. Give an example of how an extreme behavior got someone you both know into trouble.

Then, tell your child an example of how you used a moderate behavior in a new situation, when you *felt* like using an extreme behavior. Write it here:

_____

_____

_____

_____

Then, ask your child for an example of how he or she tried a moderate behavior in a new situation, even when he or she *felt* like using an extreme behavior. Help your child think of an example if he or she cannot. Write the example here:

_____

_____

_____

_____

Suggest a new moderate behavior you and your child can try together. Start with something simple, like trying a new board game or going to a new park together. Talk about how it sometimes feels exciting to try something new and other times it feels uncomfortable to try something new. If you and your child have not done a new activity together in a long time, talk about small, moderate steps you might take to accomplish this. Write the new activity here, along with the moderate steps to get started. Discuss the hurdles that might come up to get in the way, and how you can overcome those hurdles.

New Activity: _____

_____

Step 1: _____

_____

Step 2: _____

_____

Step 3: _____

_____

Hurdles: _____

_____

Session 2: Hearing Your Child's Concerns

During this session, the goal is to hear your child's concerns about the separation or divorce. This is an opportunity to use your own skills of *flexible thinking* about what you hear; to *manage your upset emotions*; and to consider *moderate behaviors* after what you have heard (even if you feel like using extreme behaviors).

It is very important that you explain to your child that the focus of this session is for you to just listen and understand. This is not a negotiation session, and it is not a session for changing the parenting schedule or creating a new schedule. It is solely focused on listening and understanding the child's concerns, and answering your child's questions if appropriate.

Your Responses

Some helpful responses to say to your child's concerns may be the following:

> Thank you for telling me how you feel.
>
> I can understand how frustrating and upsetting our separation or divorce must be for you.
>
> You are not at all responsible for our separation or divorce.
>
> You are not responsible for my upset feelings—I am, and I am learning to manage them.
>
> I will think about your concerns before we talk at our next meeting (which will be about trying new ways and moderate behaviors for both of us).

Avoid Questions

Avoid asking your child a lot of specific questions. Leave it up to the child to tell you what is important to him or her. Just say "tell me more" to get them talking more, without directing them. You will get more useful information this way.

However, if you have one question you really want to ask, discuss it with the Parent-Child Counselor first. If the Counselor believes it is appropriate for this session, he or she will let you know a good time to ask your question.

Managing Your Emotions

Remember to manage your own upset emotions. Expect that your child's concerns may be upsetting to hear, so give yourself some encouraging words. When children tell their parents upsetting information, it means that they trust their parent(s) enough to share all feelings, positive and negative. When children express no negative feelings, it means that they do not feel safe, since all children have some negative feelings.

Write down 3 of the most important concerns your child has about the separation or divorce. If you have more than one child, write something about each child's concerns, as they may be different:

1. _____

_____

_____

2. _____

_____

_____

3. _____

_____

_____

_____

Write what you said in response to let your child know you heard his/her concerns:

_____

_____

_____

_____

_____

_____

_____

_____

Session 3: Teaching Your Child Skills for Resiliency

This session is designed for one or two parents at the same meeting with the child/ren. If you have made agreements about how you will make decisions, communicate and schedule time with the children, agree on how you are going to present these to the children before this meeting. If you have not made these agreements yet, see if you can before this meeting. If not, then present what agreements there are to your children and explain how the future decisions will be made (court, mediation, collaborative, negotiated by attorneys, parenting coordinator, etc.).

Before proceeding, you may find it helpful to re-read the article in Appendix E: Don't Use "Force." on page 61.

The two goals of this session are:

1. To explain the new ways that you and the other parent are going to make decisions, communicate, and spend time with your child in the new way your family is organized.

2. To discuss having your child try some new, moderate behaviors with each parent.

This can be a fun discussion or a serious discussion, and should be presented in an age-appropriate manner. If it would be beneficial, you can meet with the Parent-Child Counselor before meeting with your child/ren.

Decision-making

Inform your child about how decisions are going to be made in the future. Explain which decisions the parents will make jointly, which you will make individually, and which decisions your child can make. If other people will be making some decisions for your family, explain who they are and how they will make these decisions (court, parenting coordinator, etc.).

Write down at least one of each type of decision here:

Parents jointly decide: _____

_____

Each parent decides: _____

_____

Child can decide: _____

_____

Others will decide: _____

_____

Discuss any questions your child has about these decisions and think of some examples of each.

Avoid negotiating who makes which decisions. Instead, explain and clarify any questions they may have. Children generally want to see that their parents are organized and in agreement, especially in a separation or divorce. Children want to know what the rules are and they usually test their parents until the rules become clear. Expect resistance to your new ways of making decisions and discuss concerns they may have about them. Tell them that you won't always *feel* like making decisions this way, but that you *think* these are good methods and will make a strong effort to stick with them.

Communication

Inform your child about how communication is going to be handled in the future. Explain how the parents will communicate about parenting schedules, changes to the schedule, finances, and activities for the children (email, phone, message book, etc.). Explain how you will communicate in an emergency. Explain how your child can communicate with each of you, such as when your child is at their other house. Explain who your child should talk to about changes in the parenting schedule, money for activities, and complaints about your parenting.

Inform your child of the following methods you and the other parent have already decided. If age appropriate, ask your child what he or she thinks should go in items 4-7 before you fill them in. Only write what you agree are appropriate answers here.

Write down how communication should occur in the future:

1. Parents will usually communicate by: _____

_____

2. In an emergency, parents will communicate by: _____

_____

3. How child should communicate with you from the other parent's house: _____

_____

4. Child should talk to you about: _____

_____

5. Child should talk to other parent about: _____

_____

6. Child should complain about you to: _____

_____

7. You should complain about child to: _____

_____

Avoid *negotiating* these methods of communication, except where appropriate (such as if the child has a good idea to add). If appropriate, make the last two items a fun discussion.

Supporting the Other Parent

Explain to your child how you and the other parent are going to support each other. Give examples of what you are going to say from time to time under each of the following:

Positive comments about each other: _____

_____

Repairing statements: _____

_____

Following each other's rules: _____

_____

Encouraging time with the other parent: _____

_____

Explain that if your child doesn't want to visit with the other parent at times, your child is still expected to go and there will be consequences if he or she doesn't go. Say that if there is a need to change the schedule, it needs to be done with the agreement of both parents.

Parenting Schedule

Explain the new parenting schedule to your child. Don't negotiate the schedule, except for specific decisions which the child can make. Ask for questions and clarifications of the schedule. Write down key aspects of the schedule here, if you wish:

If the parenting schedule is going to be decided by someone else, such as a judge, explain at an age-appropriate level how these decisions will be made and when.

Trying New Moderate Behaviors

This discussion should focus on ways you can support your child in new activities with yourself and with the other parent. It is helpful to explain to your child that trying new behaviors is often confusing, scary, and we have a natural resistance to change. Yet, new behaviors can also help us learn about life, can help us develop new skills, and help us have new, exciting experiences we didn't know we could have. This is not a negotiation session and not a session for changing the parenting schedule or creating a new schedule. It is focused on *what new behaviors* you will try together, and *how* you will do them. Focus on the specifics and try to make it fun.

Think of new places to eat, fun places to go, new books to read or discuss, new games you might try, something you could build, something you could buy, etc. Ask your child for ideas of new things to do together.

Write down 3 easy new things you can do together that you have never done before:

1. _____

2. _____

3. _____

Write down 3 hard new things you can do together that you have never done before:

1. _____

2. _____

3. _____

Now, jointly pick a realistic new activity you will do together and write down when, where and how you will do it.

_____

_____

_____

New Behaviors with the other Parent

Discuss with your child activities in the past when they enjoyed being with the other parent. If they cannot think of anything, describe activities you saw them enjoying together.

Write down 3 activities your child/ren previously enjoyed doing with the other parent:

1. _____

2. _____

3. _____

Discuss with your child/ren new realistic activities they can try with the other parent. It is important to present these with a positive tone of voice, as they will pick up any negativity.

Write 3 activities your child/ren can enjoy or learn from while being with the other parent:

1. _____

_____

2. _____

_____

Tell or ask your child how you can support him or her doing activities with the other parent. **Write down your child's suggestions.** If your child resists or refuses to do anything with the other parent, explain the importance of your child trying moderate behaviors for his or her own benefit. If necessary, explain what the consequences are if he or she does not make any effort to try to be with the other parent.

Ways you can support your child spending time with the other parent:

_____

_____

_____

Write anything else you want to say to your child at this time:

_____

_____

_____

Finish by saying three things about your child that make you proud and write them here:

1. _____

2. _____

3. _____

CONGRATULATIONS!

YOU HAVE FINISHED STEP 3 OF NEW WAYS FOR FAMILIES!

APPENDICES

APPENDIX A

Responding to Hostile Mail (B.I.F.F.)

By Bill Eddy, LCSW, ESQ.

© 2008 High Conflict Institute

Hostile mail – especially email – has become much more common over the past decade. Most of this mail is just "venting," and has little real significance. However, when people are involved in a formal conflict (a divorce, a workplace grievance, a homeowners' association complaint, etc.) there may be more frequent hostile mail. There may be more people involved and it may be exposed to others or in court. Therefore, how you respond to hostile mail may impact your relationships or the outcome of a case.

Do you need to respond?

Much of hostile mail does not need a response. Letters from (ex-) spouses, angry neighbors, irritating co-workers, or attorneys do not usually have legal significance. The letter itself has no power, unless you give it power. Often, it is emotional venting aimed at relieving the writer's anxiety. If you respond with similar emotions and hostility, you will simply escalate things without satisfaction, and just get a new piece of hostile mail back. In most cases, you are better off not responding. However, some letters and emails develop power when copies are filed in a court or complaint process – or simply get sent to other people. In these cases, it may be important to respond to inaccurate statements with accurate statements of fact. If you need to respond, I recommend a B.I.F.F. response: Be Brief, Informative, Friendly and Firm.

BRIEF

Keep your response brief. This will reduce the chances of a prolonged and angry back and forth. The more you write, the more material the other person has to criticize. Keeping it brief signals that you don't wish to get into a dialogue. Just make your response and end your letter. Don't take their statements personally and don't respond with a personal attack. Avoid focusing on comments about the person's character, such as saying he or she is rude, insensitive, or stupid. It just escalates the conflict and keeps it going. You don't have to defend yourself to someone you disagree with. If your friends still like you, you don't have to prove anything to those who don't.

INFORMATIVE

The main reason to respond to hostile mail is to correct inaccurate statements which might be seen by others. "Just the facts" is a good idea. Focus on the accurate statements you want to make, not on the inaccurate statements the other person made. For example: "Just to clear things up, I was out of town on February 12th, so I would not have been the person who was making loud noises that day."
Avoid negative comments. Avoid sarcasm. Avoid threats. Avoid personal remarks about the other's intelligence, ethics or moral behavior. If the other person has a "high-conflict personality," you will have no success in reducing the conflict with personal attacks. While most people can ignore personal attacks or might think harder about what you are saying, high-conflict people feel they have no choice but to respond in anger – and keep the conflict going. Personal attacks rarely lead to insight or positive change.

FRIENDLY

While you may be tempted to write in anger, you are more likely to achieve your goals by writing in a friendly manner. Consciously thinking about a friendly response will increase your chances of getting a friendly – or neutral – response in return. If your goal is to end the conflict, then being friendly has the greatest likelihood of success. Don't give the other person a reason to get defensive and keep responding.

This does not mean that you have to be overly friendly. Just make it sound a little relaxed and non-antagonistic. If appropriate, say you recognize their concerns. Brief comments that show your empathy and respect will generally calm the other person down, even if only for a short time.

FIRM
In a non-threatening way, clearly tell the other person your information or position on an issue. (For example: "That's all I'm going to say on this issue.") Be careful not to make comments that invite more discussion, unless you are negotiating an issue or want to keep a dialogue going back and forth. Avoid comments that leave an opening, such as: "I hope you will agree with me that ..." This invites the other person to tell you "I *don't agree*."

Sound confident and don't ask for more information, if you want to end the back-and-forth. A confident-sounding person is less likely to be challenged with further emails. If you get further emails, you can ignore them, if you have already sufficiently addressed the inaccurate information. If you need to respond again, keep it even briefer and do not emotionally engage. In fact, it often helps to just repeat the key information using the same words.

Example
Joe's email: "Jane, I can't believe you are so stupid as to think that I'm going to let you take the children to your boss' birthday party during my parenting time. Have you no memory of the last six conflicts we've had about my parenting time? Or are you having an affair with him? I always knew you would do anything to get ahead! In fact, I remember coming to your office party witnessing you making a total fool of yourself – including flirting with everyone from the CEO down to the mailroom kid! Are you high on something? Haven't you gotten your finances together enough to support yourself yet, without flinging yourself at every Tom, Dick and Harry? ..." [And on and on and on.]

Jane: "Thank you for responding to my request to take the children to my office party. Just to clarify, the party will be from 3-5 on Friday at the office and there will be approximately 30 people there – including several other parents bringing school-age children. There will be no alcohol, as it is a family-oriented firm and there will be family-oriented activities. I think it will be a good experience for them to see me at my workplace. Since you do not agree, then of course I will respect that and withdraw my request, as I recognize it is your parenting time." [And that's the end of her email.]

Comment: Jane kept it brief, and did not engage in defending herself. Since this was just between them, she didn't need to respond. If he sent this email to friends, co-workers or family members (which high-conflict people often do), then she would need to respond to the larger group with more information, such as the following:

Jane: "Dear friends and family: As you know, Joe and I had a difficult divorce. He has sent you a private email showing correspondence between us about a parenting schedule matter. I hope you will see this as a private matter and understand that you do not need to respond or get involved in any way. Almost everything he has said is in anger and not at all accurate. If you have any questions for me personally, please feel free to contact me and I will clarify anything I can. I appreciate your friendship and support." [And that's it: B.I.F.F.]

Conclusion
Whether you are at work, at home or elsewhere, a B.I.F.F. response can save you time and emotional anguish. The more people who handle hostile mail in such a manner, the less hostile mail there will be.

Erica and Connor

Write a B.I.F.F. response for Erica to Connor based on the email exchange below:

Erica: "I suggest that we get a valuation of your pension, so that we can see if we should divide it, or you could have it all in exchange for another asset of equal value that goes to me. Let me know your thoughts on this. Thanks."

Connor: "That pension is mine and you're not getting a penny of it!! If you go after MY pension, I will force the sale of the house. Then where would you and the kids live? You're a fool if you think that I worked so hard all these years and now I'm going to give you support AND my pension! I will quit my job before I give you a penny of MY pension!!!"

Erica: "_____

_____

_____

_____

_____

_____ "

Discuss your response with your counselor.

FAMILY TEAM SUPPORT:
POSITIVE VS. NEGATIVE ADVOCATES

Adapted from previous works by Bill Eddy, LCSW, ESQ.
© 2019 High Conflict Institute

Most people, even those considered to be high conflict, can manage their issues and make good decisions if they have the support of reasonable people.

NEGATIVE ADVOCATES

People who think they are helping, but really make matters worse. They have gotten emotionally "hooked". They react without always knowing all the facts but feel they need to protect their loved one because they see the other parent as the "one to blame."

GENERAL CHARACTERISTICS OF A NEGATIVE ADVOCATE

- Are emotionally hooked into the situation
- Want to help, but often unintentionally escalate the situation
- Often uninformed about all the details and are often surprised to later learn that their loved one also made mistakes
- Sometimes choose to distance themselves once they hear both sides
- May get turned off when they don't agree with their loved one's position
- Often encourage their loved one from eliminating the other parent from the child's life

POSITIVE ADVOCATES

People who support the parents and children with encouragement, caring, information and ideas. They do not take sides; but suggest reasonable options and are careful not to do more work than their loved one.

GENERAL CHARACTERISTICS OF A POSITIVE ADVOCATE

- Avoid making assumptions or taking "sides"
- Investigate problems
- Provide support and information
- Avoid taking too much responsibility for other's behaviors or problems

Making Proposals

By Bill Eddy, LCSW, ESQ.

© 2010 High Conflict Institute

Any problem in the past can be turned into a proposal about the future. Proposals don't have to be complicated. You can just blurt one out during a conversation with anyone or during a meeting with any group. Proposals get attention, because they are solutions to past problems by focusing on the future. Most of us are relieved to talk about the future, rather than what we've done wrong in the past. On the other hand, most of us easily slip into talking about the past – or even get stuck talking about the past – including what everyone else has done wrong. This article focuses on how to make proposals in a way that is easy and can be done at any time.

WHAT'S IN A PROPOSAL?

Ideally, proposals will include:

Who does

What

When and

Where

For example: "I propose that you be the one who picks up Johnny after school and takes him to his soccer practice. Then, you can keep him overnight and bring him back to school the next morning."

This is much better than saying: "You never took Johnny to any of his soccer practices. You always left it up to me. Then you showed up on Saturday at his games and made it look like you were such an involved parent. I want some respect here for all that I've done!" And then the other parent attacks back: "You never gave me a chance...." And on and on.

Can you see how it would have been so much simpler to just ask for what you wanted in the future by making a proposal? It saves all of the blame and defensiveness that people get stuck in talking about the past.

So proposals are always about the future. They are not about the past or about the other person's intentions or *Why* they made the proposal. *Why* questions easily turn into a judgment about the person's proposal. "*Why* did you say that?" It really means: "I think that's a bad idea." And of course, if you think a proposal is a bad idea, then the best thing to do is to make another proposal – until you can both agree on something.

PROPOSING SOLUTIONS TO PROBLEMS

Most problems have many solutions. For example, here are some:

In a divorce dispute: "If you're going to be late after work all the time to pick up the kids on Fridays, then I propose we just change the pickup time to a more realistic time. Instead of 5pm, let's make it 6:30pm."

And the other person might propose: "I'm going to talk to my boss and see if I can get out earlier on Fridays. I'll let you know in a week. If not, then I'll agree to your proposal. If I can, then let's just leave it the way it's scheduled now."

Or in a workplace dispute: "I propose that we talk to our manager about finding a better cubicle for you, since you have so many phone calls that need to be made and I often hear them."

And the other person might propose: "I can try to make my phone calls when you're away from your cubicle. I know you're in and out. Are there any regular times that you're away each day?"

These people can keep making proposals back and forth until they can agree on something. If each proposal takes into account what the other person was concerned about, then there is a good chance for success. It's just a matter of time before they can fit their concerns together.

IT NEVER HURTS TO ASK SERIOUS QUESTIONS ABOUT A PROPOSAL

After one person has made a proposal, the other person may not be sure whether they can agree or not. Therefore, it often helps to ask questions. One of the best questions is to ask "What would your proposal look like in action?" This way you can better understand the Who, What, Where and When of the proposal. You might even ask: "What's your picture of how this would work? What would you do? What would I do, if you could picture your proposal actually happening?"

But of course, you don't want to ask *Why* questions, because that usually starts up the defensiveness. And as we know from the last class information, if someone's defensiveness is triggered, then it makes it hard for them to think of solutions to problems. *Why* questions are usually really criticisms, not questions.

Responding with YES, NO, or I'LL THINK ABOUT IT

Once you've heard a proposal and asked any questions about it, all you have to do to respond to such a proposal is say: "Yes." "No." or "I'll think about it." You always have the right to say: "Yes." "No." or "I'll think about it." Of course, there are consequences to each choice, but you always have these three choices at least. Here are some examples of each:

YES: "Yes, I agree. Let's do that." And then stop! No need to save face, evaluate the other person's proposal, or give the other person some negative feedback. Just let it go. After all, if you have been personally criticized or attacked, it's not about you. Personal attacks are not problem solving. They are about the person making the hostile attack. You are better off to ignore everything else.

NO: "No, I don't want to change the pickup time. I'll try to make other arrangements to get there on time. Let's keep it as is." Just keep it simple. Avoid the urge to defend your decision or criticize the other person's idea. You said no. You're done. Let it drop.

I'LL THINK ABOUT IT: "I don't know about your proposal, but I'll think about it. I'll get back to you tomorrow about your idea. Right now I have to get back to work. Thanks for making a proposal." Once again, just stop the discussion there. Avoid the temptation to discuss it at length, or question the validity of the other person's point of view. It is what it is.

When you say "I'll think about it," you are respecting the other person. It calms people down to know you are taking them seriously enough to think about what they said. This doesn't mean you will agree. It just means you'll think about it.

MAKE A NEW PROPOSAL: After you think about it, you can always make a new proposal. Perhaps you'll think of a new approach that neither of you thought of before. Try it out. You can always propose anything. (But remember there are consequences to each proposal.) And you can always respond: "Yes." "No." or "I'll think about it." (And there are consequences to each of those choices, too.)

AVOID MAKING IT PERSONAL

In the heat of the conflict, it's easy to react and criticize the other person's proposals—or even to criticize the other person personally, such as saying that he or she is arrogant, ignorant, stupid, crazy or evil. It's easy and natural to want to say: "You're so stupid it makes me sick." Or: "What are you, crazy?" "Your proposal is the worst idea I have ever heard." But if you want to end the dispute and move on, just ask for a proposal and respond "Yes" "No" or "I'll think about it."

Proposal Exercise

Sharing a 4-Year-Old

William and Natasha need to develop a shared parenting plan for their four-year-old daughter, Halle. They have each read articles that say different things about the best parenting plan. Natasha has read that children up to age 3 or older should have the stability of one primary parent, with the active involvement of the other parent.

William has read an article that says that adult children of divorce wished their fathers had been more involved, and it recommended sharing parenting 50-50. But it seemed to be written about older children, at least 5 years old and maybe even older than 10.

They also both were told by a Family Mediator that the best plan is always one that both parents can agree upon. The children should feel that their schedule is normal and routine, and that their parents aren't always stressed out or fighting over the schedule. Neither William nor Natasha wants to keep fighting about this.

Here are their initial proposals:

Natasha's First Proposal: *"I read an article that says its best for young children to have one primary household, but that the other parent is involved every week. So I propose that Halle live with me most of the time, but that she spends one day and overnight each week with you. In my proposal you would also have half of the major holidays each year, and then we could alternate the following year."*

William's Question: *"I have a question about your proposal. What day and overnight were you picturing that I would have each week?"*

Natasha: *"I was thinking you'd have Friday nights and all day Saturdays each week."*

William's Response: *"Ok, I think I understand your proposal. I would say No to that, as I read an article that says that it's best for children to have approximately equal time with each parent."*

William's First Proposal: *"I propose that she spend 6 days and nights with me in a two-week period, so you would have 8 nights in the same period, as I recognize she's been with you more of the time up to now. After she's five, I'd like a 50-50 schedule, so this would be a transition."*

Natasha's Question: *"Which nights would you be thinking of having with her?"*

William: *"I'd like a weekday overnight every week – like Wednesdays – and I would alternate weekends Friday at 5pm through Monday morning back to daycare one weekend and Friday overnight the other weekend."*

Natasha's Response: *"Well, my answer to that would be No. I think she's way too young to be spending that much time away from me, as I've been her primary caregiver for all these years. And that just seems like too much back and forth for a girl that young. However, I might be willing to consider a little more time, especially as she gets older.*

William: *"But I want to be fully involved in her growing up – weekdays with her schoolwork as well as weekends. So here's another proposal:*

Write a proposal for William here that you think they both could agree to:

William's Second Proposal:

These are at least 3 possible proposals for William to make now. No one proposal is right for everyone's situation, and there is usually more than one solution to a problem. Here are a few:

Option 1: 3 nights/11 nights in two weeks

William's New Proposal: *"I would agree to have three nights every two weeks. I would have Wednesdays overnight every week and Friday night and all day Saturday every other week.*

Option 2: 4 nights/10 nights in two weeks

William's New Proposal: *"I would agree to have four nights every two weeks. I would have Wednesdays overnight every week and alternate weekends from Friday at 5pm to Sunday at 5pm."*

Option 3: 5 nights/9 nights in two weeks

William's New Proposal: *"I would agree to have five nights every two weeks. I would have Wednesdays overnight every week and alternate weekends from Friday at 5pm to Monday back to school."*

Some parents would agree on Option 1, some on Option 2 and others on Option 3. The reality is that there is not a huge difference between these options. William and Natasha could go back and forth asking questions of each other and making proposals until they reach an agreement – with the assistance of a mediator, collaborative professionals, a therapist or lawyers. The idea is that the process of making proposals helps build an agreement that can end up working the best for the people involved. Be patient and creative, and you can probably come up with a good solution.

APPENDIX D

Is Your Child Alienated?

By Bill Eddy, LCSW, ESQ.

IS YOUR CHILD REJECTING ONE PARENT?   In divorce or separation, 10% - 15% of children express strong resistance to spending time with one of their parents – and this may be increasing in our society. It may be the father or mother. It may be the parent the child "visits," or the parent where the child lives. Is this the result of abuse by the "rejected" parent? Or is this the result of alienation by the "favored" parent? The idea that one parent can alienate a child against the other has been a big controversy in family courts over the past 20 years, with the conclusion that there are many possible causes for this resistance. Most courts take reports of alienation very seriously and want to know if this is the result of abuse or alienating behavior. Resistance to spending time with a parent is always a serious problem. This needs to be investigated, fully understood, and treated with counseling in many cases. Otherwise, the child's future relationships may be much more difficult.

IS THIS THE RESULT OF ABUSE?   The first concern of the courts is protecting the children. If there are reports of child abuse as the cause of the child's alienated behavior, the judge may make a protective order restraining contact with the "rejected" parent, such as a temporary order for supervised visitation. If you are the "rejected" parent you may feel that supervised visitation is unnecessary or insulting. Yet this may be your biggest help, as someone neutral can observe the child's behavior and your relationship. Often the judge will say that he or she will not make any assumptions and wants more information before understanding the cause.

IS THIS THE RESULT OF "PARENTAL ALIENATION SYNDROME?"   It is important to know that the courts across the country have not adopted the idea that there is such a syndrome. A syndrome requires a generally accepted cause and effect, and there are many possible causes of children's alienated behavior (abuse by a parent, alienating behavior by a parent, lack of emotional boundaries by a "rejected" parent, lack of emotional boundaries by a "favored" parent, developmental stage, outside influences, etc.). Also, despite alienating behavior by some parents, many children are not resistant to spending time with the other parent. So it is not accepted as a syndrome. However, the courts generally recognize that some children are alienated – they just don't know the reason automatically and often want more information.

WHAT ARE THE SIGNS OF AN ALIENATED CHILD?   Children who are not abused, but are alienated have emotionally intense feelings but vague or minor reasons for them. A child might say: "I won't go to see my father!" Yet she might struggle to find a reason: "He doesn't help me with my homework." Or: "He dresses sloppy." Or: "He just makes me angry all the time." Another child might say: "I hate my mother!" Yet again the reasons are vague or superficial: "She's too controlling." "She doesn't understand me like my dad." These children complain that they are afraid of the other parent, yet their behavior shows just the opposite – they feel confident in blaming or rejecting that parent without any fear or remorse. Some of them speak negatively of the "rejected" parent to others, then relax when they are with the "rejected" parent. Others run away, rather than spend time with the rejected parent. All of these behaviors are generally different from those of truly abused children, who are often extra careful not to offend an abusive parent, are often hesitant to disclose abuse and often recant even though it's true.

WHY DO ALIENATED CHILDREN FEEL SO STRONGLY?   Alienated children generally show intensely negative emotions and an absence of ambivalence. New research on the brain suggests that this may be the result of the unconscious and nonverbal transfer of negative emotions from parent to child. The parent's intense angry outbursts (even if they are rare), intense sadness, and intensely negative statements about the other parent may be absorbed unconsciously by the child's brain, without the child even realizing it. The child then develops intensely negative emotions toward the other parent (or anyone the upset parent dislikes), but doesn't consciously know why. This may explain the vague or minor reasons given by alienated children for intensely rejecting a good parent. This spilling over of negative emotions from upset parent to child may have begun years before the divorce, so that the child is very tuned in to the upset parent, and automatically and instantly absorbs their emotions and point of view.

DOES CUSTODY MAKE A DIFFERENCE? If one parent has almost all of the parenting time, then the child will not have his or her own experiences with the other parent to know that he or she is not bad. Most states expect children to have substantial time with both parents – except in cases of abuse. Ironically, the amount of time is generally not the biggest factor. The biggest factor is if one parent is constantly spilling over intensely negative emotions to the child about the other parent, while the other parent is following court orders and not addressing these issues at all. For this reason, children can become alienated against either a non-custodial parent or a custodial parent. This can be either the father or the mother. It's like a bad political campaign, with one side campaigning hard and the other side not campaigning at all.

HOW CAN YOU PREVENT ALIENATION? You might be alienating your child against the other parent or against yourself, without even being conscious of it - especially during a divorce. Here are seven suggestions:

1. POSITIVE COMMENTS: Regularly point out positive qualities of the other parent to your child.
2. REPAIRING COMMENTS: All parents make negative comments about the other parent at times. If you realize you made such a comment, follow up with a "repairing comment": "I just spoke negatively about your father [or mother]. I don't really mean to be so negative. He has many positive qualities and I really value your relationship with him. I'm just upset and my feelings are my responsibility, not his and not yours."
3. AVOID REINFORCING NEGATIVE COMMENTS: Healthy children say all kinds of things, positive and negative, about their parents – even about abusive parents. If there is abuse, have it investigated by professionals. If not, be careful that you are not paying undue attention to their negative comments and ignoring their positive comments.
4. TEACH PROBLEM-SOLVING STRATEGIES: If your child complains about the other parent's behavior, unless it is abusive, suggest strategies for coping: "Honey, tell your father something nice before you ask for something difficult." "Show your mother the project you did again, she might have been busy the first time." "If he/she is upset, maybe you can just go to your room and try not to listen and draw a picture instead."
5. AVOID EXCESSIVE INTIMACY: Children naturally become more independent and self-aware as they grow up. Be careful not to be excessively intimate with your child for the child's age, as this may create an unhealthy dependency on you. Examples include having the child regularly sleep with you in your bed beyond infancy; sharing adult information and decisions (such as about the divorce); and excessive sadness at exchanges or how you miss the child when he or she is at the other parent's house.
6. AVOID EXCESSIVE COMPARISONS: When you emphasize a skill or characteristic that you have, don't place it in comparison to weaknesses of the other parent. You each have different skills and qualities that are important to your child. By comparing yourself positively and the other parent negatively (even if this feels innocent), you can inadvertently influence your child. Remember that your child is a combination of both of you, and thinking negatively of one parent means the child may think negatively about half of himself or herself.
7. GET SUPPORT OR COUNSELING FOR YOURSELF: It is impossible to go through a divorce without getting upset some of the time. Protect your child from as much as possible by sharing your upset feelings with adult friends and family, away from your child. Get counseling to cope with the stress you are under.

WILL THE COURT ADDRESS THIS ISSUE? Routinely, in a divorce or separation, the court will order that neither parent shall make disparaging remarks about the other parent within hearing of the child. Some courts may ask you for 3 positive comments about the other parent or 3 steps you are taking to protect the child from absorbing your negative emotions toward the other parent. Think about this seriously, so that you are prepared to answer this question if it is raised. Most of all, practice the suggestions described above.

Don't Use Force

By Bill Eddy, LCSW, Esq.

© 2009 High Conflict Institute

"I won't force the children to go with the other parent," is one of the statements I hear sometimes from parents going through a separation or divorce. This statement has become so common (three times in one day recently), that I decided a short article on this subject would be helpful.

Expectations

Parents have a lot of expectations for their children, for their own benefit. You expect them to go to school. You expect them to do their homework. You expect them to come home at night. You expect them to brush their teeth. You expect them to do their chores. You expect them not to swear in public. You expect them not to have sex. You expect them not to use drugs, etc., etc.

We use all of our resources to "force" them to do (or not do) these things. But we don't use the word "force" with these activities. We use the word "expect." A positive word for their long-term benefit, rather than a negative word. And your children get the message. So try not to use the word "force," with all its negativity. Instead, use the positive word "expect." "I expect you to go with your mother/father – we both expect that."

It's Not an Option

Of course, children will resist doing a negative option. They don't want to see the dentist. They don't want to go to school on some days. Even parents don't want to go to work on some days. But most of us go to work anyway, because we need to get paid. It's not an option to stay home.

Somehow, children get the message that going to the other parent's house after a separation or divorce is optional. If you give them a choice and imply it will be a negative experience, any healthy child is going to want to avoid it. Since children have so few options in their lives, if you give them an option to avoid something negative, they will avoid it.

Children Don't Like Moving

Most of the time, children like being where they are. When given a choice, many children who live in two households would rather stay where they are at the moment. It doesn't mean that they don't want to see their Mom or Dad, it just means that they don't want to stop what they're doing, get up, pack up, and go somewhere else. Once they get to the other house, they act just the same way. Don't take it personally: most of the time children just prefer where they are and what they're doing. They live in the present.

Use Positive and Negative Consequences

If children don't do the things that we expect, we usually use consequences with them rather than physically picking them up and taking them. This is especially true with teenagers. Instead, we take away privileges or give new opportunities when they succeed.

Take school, for example. If your child refuses to go to school, do you: Take them out for ice cream? Spend more personal time and attention with them? Take them shopping or to the movies? Allow them to watch TV all day? Surf the internet? If you do, do you think they would increasingly stay away from school? Of course. I have worked with families where this occurred. Instead, if a child resists spending time with the other parent without a very good reason, use the same consequences you would use if they refused to go to school. And don't blame it on the other parent – just be matter-of-fact. In a separation or divorce, attitude is everything.

Avoid Assumptions

In a separation or divorce, it's easy to misinterpret a child's resistance to spending time with one of the parents. It may be about something very minor and the child will change his or her mood soon, unless you give this mood excessive attention or power.

It is easy for a parent to jump to the conclusion that the child has the exact same thoughts about the other parent, such as complicated anger about adult issues that the child may not know about or understand. Or you may be concerned that your child's sadness or anger toward the other parent may mean he or she has been abused or treated badly. While these things could be true, be careful to check them out without making assumptions.

Emotions are Contagious

On the other hand, children do absorb their parent's emotions. It's an important part of how they learn about life, and how they stay connected to their parents. Recent brain research explains how "mirror neurons" cause children to mirror their parents' emotions, as well as behavior. So your child may have picked up your intense emotions about the separation or divorce, and show the exact same fear, sadness, or anger – yet have no logical explanation for it. While it may seem like the child has the same feelings and thoughts that you do, your child may actually just have the same feelings – your feelings.

So be careful not to let your child see or hear your upset feelings about the other parent. Arguments or physical confrontations between parents that are observed by a child can be particularly distressing for a child and may increase their resistance to one parent. Children need to be protected from their parents' behavior sometimes.

Get Family Counseling

If a child develops a resistance to spending time with one parent, it is potentially a serious problem which needs to be treated sooner rather than later. If there is a child abuse issue, it needs to be addressed and stopped. If there has been domestic violence (an incident or a pattern), then this is an important problem to be treated, rather than ignored. Children may be the first to show a problem which needs family attention. And if it is a child absorbing a parent's negative emotions about the separation or divorce, this also needs to get addressed and resolved.

Often the best approach is for a counselor to meet with each parent and the child or children before resistance turns into refusal. And if a child is refusing to see a parent, then it is even more important to take this approach as soon as possible. By meeting with both parents at separate times with the child or children, parents can help and support each other in helping their child. Getting an individual counselor for the child is less effective.

Conclusion

Maybe you can't "force" a child to spend time today with one parent. But you can have consequences, investigate the situation, and get the help of a family counselor. In the long run, it will be better for all of you.

The NEW WAYS Parent-Child Talk

By Bill Eddy, LCSW, ESQ.

When parents separate, having a talk with your children that includes some or all of the following may be helpful (presented in age-appropriate terms). You can say this separately or jointly to your children. It helps if you agree on when you are going to say this to them, and what details you have agreed upon to tell them. For example: parenting schedule, how you will communicate, and how decisions will be made.

1. New ways in different houses: We're going to be organizing our family in new ways from now on. Your mother/father and I are going to be living in different houses and bringing new people into our lives. While we are separating or getting a divorce, we are not separating from you. We will both do everything we can to keep our relationships with you loving and strong. You deserve the best from both of us.

2. Positive ways with each other: We're going to try to act in positive ways with each other. We're going to encourage you to have a strong relationship with both of us. We're going to avoid comparing ourselves to each other, by saying one of your parents is a better person than the other. We both have made mistakes and I am working on myself to be a better person in my life. And we both have strengths that you can learn from, and I will remind you of your mothers'/father's strengths in case you forget occasionally.

3. Avoiding extreme behaviors: As we organize your family in new ways, we are going to try to avoid extreme behaviors by using moderate behaviors, because families are hurt by extreme behaviors. If your mother/father does something extreme, I am still going to try to use moderate behaviors. Because one extreme behavior does not deserve another.

4. Managing our emotions: I am going to try to manage my own emotions as we go through this separation or divorce. You are not responsible for the separation or divorce, and you are not responsible for my feelings. I alone am responsible for how I manage my emotions and for protecting you from my most intense emotions. This will be a hard time and I will not be perfect.

5. Emotions can be contagious: I understand that emotions can be contagious, so I will try to reassure you that you do not have to have my emotions. You are a separate person and will have your own emotions about this separation or divorce. You should always feel free to talk about your feelings with me and I will respect your feelings, even when they are different from mine. The most important thing is that I will try to do my best to let you continue to be a child while I continue to be a parent.

6. Flexible thinking: I am going to use flexible thinking in handling our separation or divorce. This means that you can approach me with any ideas about what you and I can do together, and about the new ways our family will be operating. But remember that your mother/father and I will be doing the decision-making. This means I will try to solve problems without getting stuck in all-or-nothing thinking where I only see one solution. There are many ways to make our lives work well together and I will be open-minded.

7. Rules in both houses: There will still be rules in each of our houses, even though some of the rules will be different. We both expect you to follow the other parent's rules when you are in the other's house.

Do you have any questions about these new ways of doing things?

VERIFICATION OF COMPLETION

NEW WAYS FOR FAMILIES: INDIVIDUAL COUNSELING

Date first contacted by parent _____

Date Received Parent's Behavioral Declaration_____

Date Received copy of court orders from parent_____

Date Received Parent's Reply Declaration_____

Date Parent attended 1st Individual Session_____

Upon completion, the Individual Counselor should copy this sheet, sign it and submit it to the client. The client may provide it to anyone he or she chooses, including other professionals and/or the court.

I hereby verify that _____ has attended at least 6 sessions of New Ways for Families: Individual Counseling of at least 45 minutes each. I hereby verify that he or she has completed all of the corresponding written assignments for 6 sessions of New Ways Individual Counseling. I believe it would be appropriate/inappropriate (circle one) for this client to proceed to New Ways for Families: Parent-Child Counseling.

_____   _____
Date   Licensed Mental Health Professional

www.HighConflictInstitute.com

VERIFICATION OF COMPLETION

NEW WAYS FOR FAMILIES: PARENT-CHILD COUNSELING

Date first contacted by parent _____

Date Received Parent's Behavioral Declaration_____

Date Received copy of court orders from parent_____

Date Received Parent's Reply Declaration_____

Date Parent attended 1st Individual Session_____

Upon completion, the Parent-Child Counselor should copy this sheet, sign it and submit it to the client. The client may provide it to anyone he or she chooses, including other professionals and/or the court.

I hereby verify that _____ has attended at least 3 sessions of Step 3 of New Ways for Families: Parent-Child Counseling of 60-90 minutes each with his or her child(ren). I hereby verify that he or she has completed all of the corresponding written assignments for 3 sessions of New Ways Parent-Child Counseling. I believe it would be appropriate/inappropriate (circle one) for _____ to proceed to Step 4 of New Ways for Families: Family (or Court) Decision-Making.

_____   _____

Date   Licensed Mental Health Professional

www.HighConflictInstitute.com

Printed in the USA
CPSIA information can be obtained
at www.ICGtesting.com
JSHW050913020424
60411JS00005B/6